DICTIONARY

Kingfisher Books, Grisewood & Dempsey Ltd,
Elsley House, 24–30 Great Titchfield Street,
London W1P 7AD

First published in 1991 by Kingfisher Books

Copyright © Grisewood & Dempsey Ltd 1991

BRITISH LIBRARY CATALOGUING IN PUBLICATION DATA
Root, Betty
    Dictionary
    1. English language
    I. Title   II. Series
423

ISBN 0 86272 720 0

Series editor: Jackie Gaff
Word-origin boxes: George Beal
Edited by: Brigid Avison
Series designer: Ben White Associates
Cover design: Terry Woodley
Cover illustration: Ian Jackson
Illustrations by: Linden Artists (Adam Hook,
Alan Male, Clive Pritchard, Sebastian Quigley,
Linda Worrall); Ian Jackson (p. 43).

Phototypeset by Southern Positives and
Negatives (SPAN), Lingfield, Surrey
Printed in Hong Kong

DICTIONARY

BETTY ROOT

Kingfisher Books

USING A DICTIONARY

Words are a very important part of our lives – without them we would not be able to describe the world around us or the things that happen to us. That is why dictionaries are really useful books. They show us how to spell words correctly and they tell us what words mean.

The words in a dictionary are arranged in a special way so that it is easy for us to find them. This special way of arranging words is called **alphabetical order**, because it follows the order of the 26 letters of the alphabet –

**a b c d e f g h i j k l m n o p
q r s t u v w x y z**

This means that all the words that begin with the letter **a** are grouped at the beginning of a dictionary. They are followed by words that begin with the letter **b**, then the letter **c**, and so on. Words that begin with **z** are at the end of the dictionary.

All the different words that start with the same letter of the alphabet are arranged according to the letters inside them, starting with the second letter. For example, **add** comes before **afraid**, and **afraid** comes before **age**. When words have the same first and

second letter, they are arranged according to the third letter. That is why **alike** comes before **alligator**.

Suppose you want to look up the word **clown**. You start by finding the words that begin with the letter **c**. **C** is near the beginning of the alphabet, so the **c**-words are near the front of the dictionary. Next you look for words that begin with the letters **cl**. Then you look at the third and fourth letters of the **cl**-words – **clown** is on page 19, after the word **cloud**.

Underneath **clown**, you will find a sentence telling you the meaning of the word. Some words also have a picture to show you what they mean, or an extra sentence to show you how they are used.

Words can be fun as well as useful. In the special boxes throughout this dictionary you can read all sorts of fascinating facts about the history of words and some of the funny ways that we use them.

Aa

absent
To be away. Anne is **absent** from school because she has a cold.

accident
Something that happens which is not expected, usually something bad.

LATIN FALL

The word **accident** came from the Latin words *ad* and *cadere*, which mean 'to fall towards'.

---

acrobat
Someone who does balancing tricks, usually in a circus.

add
1 To put one thing with another.
2 To find the total of two or more numbers. If you **add** two and two, you get four.

address
Where a place is – its number or name, and the names of the street, the town and sometimes the country.

admire
To think well of something or somebody.

adult
A grown-up. Children grow up to be **adults**.

adventure
Something exciting and sometimes dangerous. Adam's **adventures** started when he went to live in the jungle.

aeroplane
A flying machine with wings and an engine. The **aeroplane** flew high above the clouds.

afraid

1 To be frightened. Alex is **afraid** of the dog because she thinks it might bite her.

2 To be sorry. I'm **afraid** I can't help you.

afternoon

The part of the day between the morning and the evening.

age

The length of time a person has lived or a thing has lasted.

air

What we breathe. **Air** is all around us – we can't see it, but we can feel it when the wind blows.

album

A special book which you can use for keeping things such as stamps or photographs.

alike

Nearly the same. My brother and I look so **alike** that people find it hard to tell us apart.

alligator

An animal with sharp teeth and a long tail, which is related to the crocodile. It lives in warm countries.

SPANISH LIZARD

Alligator came from the Spanish el *lagarto*, meaning 'the lizard'. The name was invented by Spanish explorers when they first came across the animal in Central America in the 1500s.

allow
To let someone do something. On Fridays and Saturdays, I am **allowed** to stay up until 10 o'clock.

alphabet
All the letters from a to z. There are 26 letters in the **alphabet**.

FROM A TO B

The word **alphabet** was based on the names of the first two letters of the Greek **alphabet** – *alpha* (α) and *beta* (β).

---

ambulance
A large van used to take sick or injured people to hospital. Amy went to the hospital in an **ambulance** after she broke her leg.

amphibian
An animal that can live on land as well as in the water. Frogs and toads are **amphibians**.

ancient
Very old or very long ago. The **ancient** Egyptians lived many thousands of years ago.

angry
Very cross or bad tempered. My dad was **angry** with me when I hit a ball through the window and broke it.

animal
A living thing that is not a plant. Human beings are **animals**, and so are elephants and mice, cats and dogs, bees and birds, fish and snakes. Unlike plants, **animals** can move about.

annoy
To make someone cross.
I **annoy** my mum when
I don't make my bed.

answer
What you want to know
when you ask someone
a question. If you ask
'What colour is snow?',
the **answer** is 'white'.

arrive
To reach a place. The
train **arrived** at the
station on time.

artist
Someone who draws or
paints pictures.

astronaut
A space traveller.

automatic
When a machine works
without people looking
after it. Our washing
machine is **automatic**
– it washes and spins
the clothes by itself.

avalanche
A sudden slide of snow
and rocks down a
mountainside.

awake
Not sleeping. I know
that she is **awake** – her
eyes are open!

awful
Very bad, nasty. The
weather is so **awful**
today that we can't go
out for a walk.

STAR TRAVELLER

The word **astronaut**
was first used in 1929.
It came from two
Greek words – *astron*,
meaning 'star', and
nautikos, meaning
'sailor'.

Bb

baby
A very young child or animal.

badger
A shy dog-sized animal, which sleeps during the day and hunts at night. Its fur is black, but it has thick white stripes on its head.

bake
To cook in an oven. You have to **bake** cakes before you can eat them.

BAKER'S DOZEN

The word dozen means 12, but there are 13 things in a baker's dozen!

balloon
A bag that floats when filled with air or gas.

HAVING A BALL

The Italians have a word *balla*, meaning 'ball', and from this came *ballone*, which is a 'great ball' – and that's what a **balloon** looks like!

bare
1 Without anything on.
2 Empty. The room looked **bare** without any furniture in it.

basket
Something for holding or carrying things in, usually made of very thin sticks twisted or woven together.

battery
A container for storing electricity. Torches and radios often run on **batteries** – they don't have to be plugged into anything.

beach
The sand or pebbles at the edge of a lake or the sea.

beak
The hard outer part of a bird's mouth.

bear
1 A large furry wild animal with strong claws and a short tail.
2 To put up with something. I can't **bear** tidying my room.

beautiful
Very pretty. Roses are **beautiful** flowers.

bee
An insect that flies and makes honey.

Beekeepers keep their **bees** in **bee**hives.

beginning
The start of something. I started the story at the **beginning** and read through to the end.

believe
To think something is true. I **believe** you because I know that you don't tell lies.

BUZZY SAYINGS

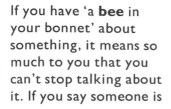

If you have 'a **bee** in your bonnet' about something, it means so much to you that you can't stop talking about it. If you say someone is 'the **bee**'s knees', you like them very much or think they are very clever. If you make 'a **bee**line' for something, you go straight for it.

bicycle

bicycle
A machine with two wheels, and pedals you turn with your feet to make the wheels go round.

bird
An animal that has wings and feathers, and which lays eggs. Most **birds** can fly.

birthday
The day you were born on. You remember it each year with presents and a cake.

blast-off
The moment a rocket leaves the ground and is launched into Space.

blood
The red liquid in your body which is pumped round by your heart.

boat
A type of small open ship used for travelling on water.

body
The whole of you, from your head to your toes.

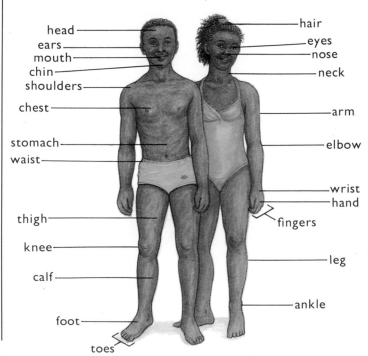

head • ears • mouth • chin • shoulders • chest • stomach • waist • thigh • knee • calf • foot • toes

hair • eyes • nose • neck • arm • elbow • wrist • hand • fingers • leg • ankle

bone
One of the hard parts inside your body that together make up your skeleton.

book
Pages of paper fastened together inside a cover. On the pages are words to read or pictures to look at.

BOOK LOVER
A **book**worm is someone who reads a lot of **books**.

borrow
When someone gives you something for a while, and you return it later. My friend Ben lets me **borrow** his bike, because I take care of it and I always return it.

bottle
A container for liquids. **Bottles** are usually made of glass or plastic.

bounce
To spring back again. Balls **bounce** when they hit the ground.

brain
The part of your body inside your head that takes care of thoughts, feelings and memory.

brave
Brave people will help others even though it may be dangerous.

The **brave** firefighter rescued the **baby** from the **burning** house.

bread
A food mainly made from flour and baked in an oven.

break
1 To smash something. If you drop that glass, it will **break** in pieces.
2 A rest. At school, we have a **break** between lessons in the morning and the afternoon.

breakfast
The first meal of the day, usually eaten early in the morning.

breathe
What you do when you take air in and out of your body.

bridge
Something built across a river, road or railway, so that we can get to the other side.

bring
To fetch or carry. I **bring** sandwiches with me to school every day.

build
To make something by putting pieces together.

bulldozer
A big machine with a large blade at the front, which is used for moving soil and rocks.

burn
To be on fire. We poured water on the **burning** wood to put it out.

burrow
A hole in the ground that was dug by an animal to use as a home.

bus
A large road vehicle which has lots of seats and can carry lots of people.

busy
Having a lot to do. I can't go out with you because I'm **busy** doing my homework.

butterfly
An insect with large thin wings, which are often beautifully patterned and coloured.

buy
To get something by giving someone money for it.

Cc

cage
A special box with bars for keeping animals in. My pet hamster lives in a **cage**.

cake
A sweet food made from flour, butter, eggs and sugar, and baked in an oven. I have a special **cake** on my birthday.

calculator
A machine that can do sums very quickly.

PEBBLE MATHS
The ancient Romans added things up by moving pebbles around on a special board. The word **calculator** came from the Latin word for a pebble – *calculus*.

calendar
A list of all the days, weeks and months of the year.

camel
An animal with a long neck and one or two humps on its back. **Camels** live in the desert and can go for a long time without water.

camera
A machine for taking photographs or for shooting films.

I used my **camera** to take photographs of a **camel** when I went to the zoo.

car
A road vehicle which is powered by an engine and steered with a wheel. Most **cars** run on petrol.

carry

carry
To take things from one place to another. I **carry** my sports gear to school with me in a bag.

cassette
A small plastic box with a special tape inside it which stores sounds and sometimes pictures as well. You put it in a **cassette** recorder to listen to music, and in a video machine to watch films recorded on a video **cassette**.

castle
A large building with thick walls and high towers, built in olden times to keep out dangerous enemies.

catch
1 Something used to hold a door or a box closed.
2 To take hold of something moving. Cats often try to **catch** birds.
3 To get an illness. I hope that I don't **catch** your cold.

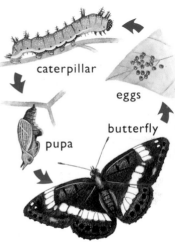

caterpillar

eggs

butterfly

pupa

caterpillar
A worm-like animal with legs, which grows up into a butterfly.

WORM OR CAT?
The word **caterpillar** came into English from the old French word *chatepelosa*, meaning 'hairy cat'.

centre
1 The middle part of anything.
2 A place specially for certain activities. I go to a sports **centre** to play football.

chase
To run after something, usually to catch it. The wind blew my hat off, so I had to **chase** after it.

cheerful
Looking or feeling happy. The circus clown painted a big smile on his face to make him look **cheerful**.

cheese
A food made from milk.

chew
To turn food over in your mouth and chop it up with your teeth.

children
Young boys or girls.

chimpanzee
A black hairy type of ape. **Chimpanzees** live in the African jungle and, like all apes, they do not have tails.

A **cheerful chimpanzee chewing** a banana.

chocolate
A sweet brown food or drink made from cocoa.

A SWEET FIND
Chocolate was not known in Europe until the 1500s, when the Spanish brought it from the country now called Mexico. It was a favourite food of the Aztec people who called it *chocolatl*.

choose
To pick one thing instead of another. I like **choosing** which clothes to wear when I get up each day.

cinema
A building in which films are shown on a big screen.

circus
A travelling show, with acrobats, clowns and animals, usually held in a big tent.

city
An important or very large town.

clean
Not dirty. After I eat a meal, I brush my teeth to **clean** them.

climb
To go up.

clock
A machine for telling the time.

clothes
All the things you wear.

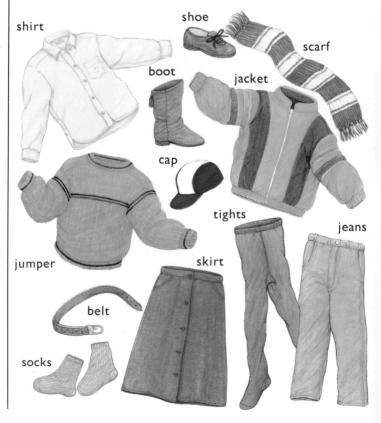

shirt

shoe

scarf

boot

jacket

cap

tights

jeans

jumper

skirt

belt

socks

cloud
A fluffy white or grey patch in the sky, made of lots of tiny drops of water. Those grey **clouds** make me think that it will rain soon.

clown
A person in a circus who does things to make people laugh.

The **clumsy clown** tripped over a **coconut**.

clumsy
Awkward. My brother is very **clumsy** – he's always breaking things.

coal
A black rock-like material which is mined from the ground and burned to give heat.

coconut
A large nut with a hard hairy shell, which has a delicious hard white food and a milky liquid inside it.

collect
To bring together. Camilla likes to **collect** stamps from different countries.

colour
Red, yellow and blue are **colours**, and so are black and white.

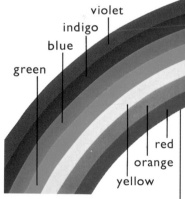

violet
indigo
blue
green
red
orange
yellow

There are seven different **colours** in a rainbow.

computer
An electronic machine that stores information and can help you to work things out quickly.

container
Something for holding or storing things in – like a jar or a box.

cook
To heat food until it is ready to eat. Mum is **cooking** soup for lunch.

cotton
A kind of plant that has soft white fluffy hairs around its seeds. The hairs are used to make **cotton** cloth and sewing thread.

ARABIC CLOTH

Cotton was brought from China and India to Europe by the Arabs, so our word comes from an Arabic one – *qutn* – which sounds very similar.

countdown
The time before blast-off, when numbers are counted backwards.

country
1 The land outside a town, where there are fields and trees.

2 A part of the world that has its own government. France and Spain are **countries**.

coward
Not brave – someone who is afraid in times of danger.

I'm a **coward** about **crabs** – they frighten me.

crab
An animal with a hard shell and ten legs, two of which have big claws.

crocodile
A large river animal with big sharp teeth and a long tail.

crowd
Lots of people in one place. There was a **crowd** outside the football ground, waiting for the gates to open.

Dd

dam
A type of wall that is built to block a flow of water. Beavers build **dams** of twigs and weed across streams.

dance
To move in time to a beat, usually to music.

dangerous
Something that can hurt or harm you. Thin ice is very **dangerous** – if it cracks you could fall into the water.

dark
Without light. It gets **dark** at night, after the Sun goes down.

dawn
The time of the morning when it begins to grow light. **Dawn** is when the Sun rises.

day
Each **day** starts at midnight and lasts until midnight. There are 24 hours in each **day**, and there are seven **days** in every week.

EARLY DAYS

Sunday was 'the day of the Sun', because people worshipped the Sun once upon a time.
Monday was the 'day of the Moon'.
Tuesday came from Tiw, or Tui, an ancient god of war.

Wednesday came from Woden, or Odin, a chief of the gods.
Thursday came from Thor, the thunder god.
Friday came from Frigg, Woden's wife.
Saturday came from the planet Saturn.

deaf
Someone who cannot hear. I shouted loudly, but the **deaf** person could not hear me.

dead
No longer alive. The plants were **dead** because it hadn't rained for weeks.

desert
Dry land where few things grow.

diary
A special book in which you write down what happens every day.

different
Not the same. I wear **different** clothes in summer and winter.

difficult
Not easy, hard to do. Patting your head and rubbing your tummy at the same time is very **difficult** to do.

dinner
The main meal of the day, often eaten in the evening.

dinosaur
A type of animal that died out millions of years ago, a long time before the first people lived on Earth.

TERRIBLE NAME

The word **dinosaur** was made up in 1841 by the scientist Richard Owen. It comes from two Greek words, *deinos* and *sauros*, which mean 'terrible lizard'.

dirty
Not clean. My clothes got **dirty** when I fell down in the mud.

disappear
To go out of sight. I couldn't see the rabbit after the magician made it **disappear**.

disco
A place where you go to dance to pop music.

dive
To go into the water headfirst. You should only **dive** in at the deep end of a swimming pool.

doctor
Someone who tries to find out what is wrong with you when you are sick, and to make you better again.

dolphin
A sea animal which looks like a large fish with a pointed mouth.

drag
To pull something along slowly. We had to **drag** the sack of wood along the ground because it was too heavy to lift.

dragon
A make-believe animal which breathes fire and has wings and claws.

dream
Pictures, sounds and thoughts that pass through your mind while you are asleep.

driver
Someone who steers a car or other vehicle.

duck
1 A bird that can swim as well as fly.
2 To bend down quickly to get out of the way.

Ee

eagle
A large fierce bird with a sharp hooked beak. **Eagles** hunt and eat other animals.

earth
1 The **Earth** is the planet on which we live.
2 The ground beneath our feet, the soil in which plants grow.

earthquake
A sudden shaking of the land, which can sometimes make the ground crack open.

easy
Not difficult, no trouble. Having a map made it **easy** to find my way.

echo
The sound you hear when a noise bounces back at you. You can usually hear an **echo** if you shout loudly in a tunnel or a cave.

electricity
A kind of power used to make heat and light, as well as to make many machines work. If you press a light switch you turn **electricity** on.

elephant
A very large animal which has big floppy ears, a long nose called a trunk, and two big teeth called tusks.

JUMBO SIZED

Ever since a circus **elephant** was named Jumbo, people have used the word to describe something very large – like a jumbo jet.

empty
Nothing inside. The bucket is **empty** – I've poured all the water out of it.

enemy
Someone who wants to harm you – the people a country fights against in a war.

energy
The power or strength to do something. We get **energy** to live and grow from the food we eat.

engine
A machine that makes things move or work. A car **engine** makes the wheels go round.

enormous
Very large, like an elephant.

escape
To get away from people or a place.

The robbers used a fast car to **escape** from the police.

evening
The part of day between the afternoon and the night-time.

exciting
Something that stirs you up and makes you feel happy. Swooping across the sky in an aeroplane is **exciting**.

exercises
Movements you do to make your body strong and fit.

Ff

factory
A building where things are made, usually with machines – for example, a car **factory**.

family
A group of people who are related to each other.

I keep photographs of my **family** in an album.

famous
Very well known. Madonna is a **famous** pop star.

farmer
Someone who uses the land to grow plants and raise animals for food.

favourite
Something or someone you like best. Blue is my **favourite** colour.

feather
One of the things that cover a bird's body. **Feathers** help to keep birds warm.

My mother and father

My aunt and uncle

My sister and brother

My grandparents

feel
1 To touch. I like to **feel** my cat's soft fur.
2 To know how you are. I **feel** happy because it's a holiday today.

female
A girl or a woman – any animal that is not male.

ferry
A boat or a ship that carries people, and cars and other vehicles, across water.

festival
A special day or time of year when people enjoy themselves. Christmas is a **festival**.

fight
When people try to hurt each other. When the teacher saw the children hitting each other, she told them not to **fight**.

film
1 The roll of special tape you put in a camera. Photographs are made from this **film**.
2 The moving picture show you see at a cinema or on television.

find
To come across something you are looking for. I lost my purse and my friend helped me to **find** it.

firefighter
A person whose job is putting out fires.

firework
Something that lets off a shower of pretty colours when it is lit, and which often makes a loud bang at the same time.

People often let off **fireworks** at **festivals** such as New Year.

fish
An animal that lives in water. A **fish** has fins and a tail to help it swim about.

flower

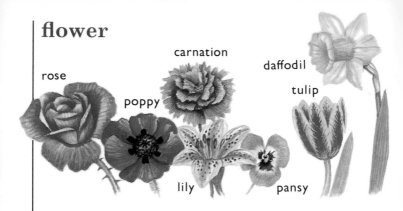

rose
carnation
daffodil
tulip
poppy
lily
pansy

flower
The coloured head of a plant. **Flowers** can be all sorts of different colours and shapes.

follow
To go after something or someone.

food
Everything we eat that helps us to stay alive and to grow.

foreign
Belonging to another country. Fiona has some **foreign** money left after her holiday in France.

FOREIGN FOREST

Foreign came from the same Latin word as **forest** did – *foris*, which means 'out of doors'.

forest
A big piece of land that is covered with lots of trees.

forget
Not to remember. If I **forget** your telephone number I won't be able to ring you.

fossil
The stony remains of an ancient plant or animal, often found inside rocks.

fox
A wild furry animal that looks like a dog.

freeze
To turn a thing into ice by making it very cold.

friend
A person you know well and like. Fred is my best **friend** – we spend lots of time together.

frightening

When something makes you afraid or worried. Sudden loud noises can be very **frightening**, especially if they wake you up in the middle of the night.

frog

A small animal that lives in and out of water. **Frogs** have long back legs to help them jump and swim.

fruit

The part of a plant that has seeds in it and which is often good to eat. Oranges, apples and grapes are different sorts of **fruit**.

full

Not empty, no room left. I couldn't get a ticket because the cinema was **full** and there weren't any seats left.

funny

1 When things make you laugh – **funny** jokes, for example.
2 Odd or strange.

furniture

The useful things we put in houses and other buildings – for example, chairs, tables, cupboards and beds.

future

The time that is to come, like tomorrow and the day after. People may live and work on the Moon in the **future**.

pear apple orange grapes lemon cherry banana tomato

Gg

game
Something you play, which usually has rules telling you what to do. There are different sorts – card **games** and ball **games**, for example.

gang
A group of friends who do things together.

garage
A place where cars are kept or mended. Our teacher's car wouldn't start, so she got a truck to tow it to the **garage** to be mended.

garden
A piece of land next to someone's house where flowers, trees, vegetables or fruit are grown.

gentle
Kind and careful. I am **gentle** with our new kitten because I don't want to hurt it.

ghost
A shadow-like shape. Some people believe that **ghosts** of dead people walk at night.

giant
A huge person or thing. Fairy stories often have a **giant** in them.

giraffe
An animal with a very long neck and long legs.

SPOTTY CAMEL?

The word **giraffe** appeared in the 1700s. Before that the animal was known as a camelopard, because people thought it looked like a cross between a camel and a leopard.

give
To hand something over.
My mum and dad **give**
me presents every year
on my birthday and at
Christmas.

glad
Pleased and happy.
Gary is **glad** that he
won first prize.

glass
1 A hard material you
can see through.
Windows have **glass** in
them.
2 Anything made of this
material, such as a
drinking **glass**.

glasses
Two pieces of special
glass which people wear
in front of their eyes to
help them see better.

goal
1 Something you aim
towards or try to do.
2 In some games, the
space between two posts
where you aim a ball to
win points.

gorilla
A wild animal, like a
large chimpanzee with a
big bullet-shaped head.

government
The person or group of
people who run a
country and make the
country's laws.

RUNNING A SHIP

The word **govern**
came from *kubernan*,
a Greek word which
means 'to steer', as
in steering a ship.

grab

grab
To take hold of something or someone quickly. If my little sister tries to run into the road, I **grab** her arm to stop her.

gravity
A planet's pulling power. The Earth's **gravity** keeps us on the ground and stops us floating off into Space.

great
1 Very large or heavy.
2 Very important or famous. It was a **great** day when people first travelled into Space.

greedy
Wanting more than you have or need.

A **greedy** man **guzzling** doughnuts.

ground
1 The surface of the Earth, the part we walk about on.
2 A sports field. I'm going to a match at the football **ground** next Saturday.

group
A number of people or things that have something in common.

grow
1 To get bigger, taller or longer. When my hair **grows**, I'm going to tie it back in a ponytail.
2 To become. The sky **grows** dark at the end of the day.

guess
To say what you think is true without really knowing. I have to **guess** the time if I'm not wearing a watch.

guzzle
To eat very quickly and greedily.

gym
Short for **gym**nasium. A room or building where people do exercises.

Hh

happy
Not sad, feeling cheerful or good. My brother is **happy** because he's just passed his driving test.

harbour
A safe place near land for ships to stay.

hate
When you really do not like someone or something. I **hate** feeling ill.

headphones
Things you put over your ears so you can listen to a radio or tape recorder without other people hearing or being annoyed by the noise.

healthy
Feeling fit and well. Fresh air and exercise make me feel very **healthy**.

heart
The part of your body that pumps blood around you.

A **helicopter** lifting a **heavy** load.

heavy
Weighing a lot. That box is far too **heavy** to lift.

helicopter
A flying machine that has spinning blades instead of wings.

help
To do something useful for someone else.

hibernate
When animals do this, they spend the winter in a kind of deep sleep.

hide
To keep out of sight or to put something out of sight. I'm going to **hide** my diary so no one can read it.

hippopotamus
A large animal with short legs, which lives in and near rivers and lakes.

holiday
Time off work or school. I'm going to the seaside for my summer **holiday** this year.

honest
An **honest** person tells the truth and does not cheat people.

honey
A sweet yellow food made by bees.

hope
To wish for something to happen. I **hope** I get a bicycle for Christmas.

horrible
Nasty or frightening. Hilary was so **horrible** to me that she made me burst into tears.

horse
A large animal with a long tail and long hair called a mane on its neck. People ride on **horses** or use them to pull things.

hospital
A building where sick people are looked after by doctors and nurses.

PIG OR HORSE?

Although it looks far more like a huge pig than a horse, the **hippopotamus** got its name from the Greek words for 'river horse'.

hotel
A special building that people pay to stay in.

hour
A length of time. There are 60 minutes in an **hour**.

house
A building where people live. Most houses have one, two or three floors or levels.

hovercraft
A vehicle that can travel over land and over water, floating on a cushion of air.

huge
Very big, enormous. His feet are so **huge** that he can't find any shoes to fit them.

hungry
Wanting to have something to eat. My tummy makes a rumbling noise when I'm **hungry**.

hunter
Someone who chases wild animals, usually to catch or kill them.

hurricane
A very violent and powerful, whirling wind or storm.

hurry
To do something quickly. My mum told me to **hurry** up because I was late for school.

hydrofoil
A boat that can travel above the surface of the water, resting on ski-like foils.

Ii

ice
Water that has frozen solid. The water in the pond turned to **ice** because the weather was so cold.

iceberg
A huge piece of ice floating in the sea. Some **icebergs** are as big as mountains.

ice-cream
A cold sweet food, rather like frozen cream.

ICE-CREAM CONE

Ice-cream cones were first made in the 1890s, by an Italian-American called Italo Marcioni.

idea
A thought or plan. Our teacher wants us to think up **ideas** for the school play.

imagine
To make a picture in your mind.

When I walk through long grass, I **imagine** I am deep in the jungle.

incredible
Difficult to believe. That's **incredible** – he peeled a banana without using his hands!

information
Facts about something. I rang the museum to get **information** about the biggest dinosaurs.

insect
A small animal with six legs, and usually two pairs of wings. Flies and ants are **insects**.

interesting
Not boring, something you want to know about. I think history is **interesting** because I like reading about the way people used to live.

invent
To make something for the very first time. I don't like making my bed – perhaps someone will **invent** a machine to do it for me!

invisible
When something cannot be seen. The spy wrote secret messages using **invisible** ink.

invite
To ask someone to go somewhere. I hope Isabel will **invite** me to her birthday party.

irrigate
To put water on dry land to help crops grow.

island
Land with water all around it.

The boat sailed away from the **island**.

itchy
When you want to scratch or rub your skin. Some flies landed on the cow's nose and made it very **itchy**.

A LOST LETTER
The word **itchy** used to start with the letter g, so a long time ago people used to say 'gitchy'!

37

Jj

jam
1 A sweet food made by boiling fruit and sugar together.
2 To push or squeeze something into a tight space. I **jammed** my clothes into the drawer.

jealous
Being unhappy because you want what others have. I was **jealous** of my brother when he was given new roller skates.

jellyfish
A sea animal whose umbrella-shaped body is seethrough and rather like clear jelly.

jewel
A pretty stone which is worth a lot of money. Diamonds, emeralds and rubies are **jewels**.

JOKE JEWELS

The word **jewel** came from the Latin word for joke – *jocus*.

jewellery
Things people wear as decoration, like earrings and necklaces.

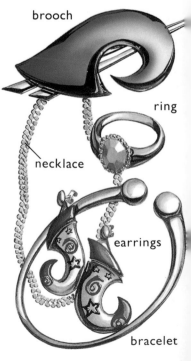

brooch

ring

necklace

earrings

bracelet

jigsaw
A puzzle game in which you fit pieces of a picture back together.

job
Something you do, your work. My mum works for the post office – her **job** is delivering letters.

join
1 To put things together. You can **join** two pieces of string by tieing them together.
2 To become a member of a group or a club.

joke
A short story told to make people laugh.

journey
Going from one place to another. The **journey** home takes us an hour.

WORK TRIP

Although today a **journey** can mean any kind of trip, it once meant 'a day's travel'. A journeyman was a skilled worker who could do 'a day's work'.

juice
The liquid you get when you squeeze fruit or crush vegetables.

jump
To leap into the air. Our dog can **jump** right over the garden fence.

jungle
A very thick forest of trees that grows in hot countries. Monkeys and tigers live in the **jungle**.

Kk

kangaroo
A large Australian animal with a long tail and two big strong back legs. Baby **kangaroos** are called joeys.

kettle
A kind of pot which is used for boiling water. A **kettle** has a lid, a handle, and a spout for pouring the water out.

kick
To hit something with your foot. Kim **kicked** the football straight into the goal.

kidnapper
Someone who steals a person and hides them away, often until money is paid to free them. The **kidnappers** wanted £100,000 before they would let the boy go.

kill
To make someone or something die. I saw our cat **kill** a mouse.

kind
1 Helpful or gentle. It was **kind** of you to help me with my homework.
2 Type or sort. A kangaroo is a **kind** of animal.

king
A man who is head of his country.

kiss
To touch someone with your lips to show that you like them.

kite
A flying toy which is made from plastic, paper or cloth stretched over a frame of light plastic, metal or wood.

knife
A tool with a handle and a sharp blade for cutting through things.

knight
Long ago, a man who lived in a castle and was ready to go to war for his king.

Knights wore armour when they fought for their **king**.

knock
To hit or bump into something very hard.
I **knocked** on the door until someone heard me and opened it.

knot
1 A way of twisting, looping and tieing string or narrow pieces of material together.
2 A small hard area in a piece of wood, where a branch once grew.

know
To be sure about something. Of course I **know** how to spell my name!

koala
A furry Australian animal which looks like a small grey bear.

41

Ll

ladder
Two long poles joined by short bars called rungs, used for climbing up things.

ladybird
A small flying beetle with spotty wing cases.

lake
A large piece of water with land all round it.

lamb
A baby sheep. **Lambs** are small and furry.

lamp
Something that shines and gives off light.

land
1 The part of the Earth's surface that is solid dry ground and which is not covered by water.
2 To arrive from the air or sea. The spaceship **landed** on the Moon.

language
The words we use to speak and write.

TONGUE TALK

The word **language** came from the French word *langue*, which means 'tongue'.

THE SAME BUT DIFFERENT

Even the same **language** can be used in different ways in different parts of the world. American and British people both speak English, but many of the words they use are very different.

American	British
apartment	flat
closet	cupboard
cookies	biscuits
elevator	lift
fall	autumn
faucet	tap
gas(oline)	petrol
vacation	holiday

Large elephants are scared of **little** mice.

large
Very big. Lisa's hat doesn't fit – it is too **large** for her head.

laser
A machine that makes a very strong and narrow beam of light – strong enough to cut metal.

lasso
A long rope with a loop at one end, used by cowboys to catch cattle.

late
Not early, past the correct time. Lee was **late** for school because he missed the bus.

laugh
A sound you make when you are happy or you see something funny. Your jokes make me **laugh**!

launch
To send a rocket into Space, or to put a boat into water.

law
A rule made by the government of a country. The **law** tells you what you can and cannot do.

lazy
Not wanting to do much. **Lazy** people don't like working.

lead
1 To go in front to show the way.
2 A strap or a chain you tie to a dog's collar to stop it running away.

learn
To find out about something or get to know how to do it. I can't play the piano, but I want to **learn**.

leather
A material made from the skin of animals, used to make things like shoes, bags and coats.

lend
To let someone use something of yours for a while.

leopard
A type of large wild cat, whose yellowy brown coat has black spot-shaped markings.

Leopards and **lions** live in Africa.

lesson
At school, a period of time you spend in class learning something.

letter
1 A written message you usually put in an envelope and send to someone.
2 One of the parts of the alphabet – a, b and c are all **letters**, for example.

library
A place where lots of books are kept. I go to the **library** every week and borrow books to read at home.

lick
To touch something with your tongue, to wet or taste it.

leopard

lion

lift

1 A special machine for carrying people or things up and down inside a building.
2 To pick up or raise something.
3 To give someone a lift is to give them a ride in a car or a lorry.

light

1 Something that shines and lets us see things, like sunlight or lamplight.
2 To make something catch fire.
3 Not heavy.
4 Not dark in colour.

lighthouse

A tall tower with a light on top which flashes to warn ships about hidden rocks and other dangers.

lightning

A flash of light you see in the sky during a thunderstorm.

A **lighthouse** lit by flashes of **lightning**.

lion

A type of large wild cat with a yellowy brown coat. Male **lions** have manes – lots of thick hair on their head, neck and shoulders.

liquid
Something like water, which flows and can be poured – not a solid.

listen
To hear something. I like **listening** to the radio when I wake up in the morning.

little
Small or tiny, not very much. I only ate a **little** chocolate – I'm saving the rest for later.

live
1 To be alive, not dead.
2 To be at home in a place. I **live** in a town, not in the country.

lizard
An animal that looks like a little snake with four legs.

Lizards live in dry lands such as deserts.

load
Something you carry or lift, usually something big or heavy.

lock
An object that is used to keep something like a door or a box shut.

lock

key

You need a key to open a **lock**.

locomotive
A machine on wheels that pulls trains.

lollipop
A big round sweet on a little stick.

lonely
Feeling sad because you are on your own. I don't like being away from my friends and family – it makes me feel **lonely**.

long

1 Not short. My trousers are so **long** I can't see my shoes.
2 To want something very much. I'm **longing** to see that new film.

look

1 To move your eyes so that you see something. You might find your ring if you **look** under the bed.
2 The way someone appears to others. You **look** very pale today.

loose

Not tight or firm. My tooth is **loose** – I think it's going to fall out.

lorry

A large road vehicle used to carry goods.

lost

When you can't find something. The dog was **lost** – it couldn't find its way home.

loud

Not quiet, noisy. Dad asked me to turn my radio down because the music was too **loud**.

love

To like something or someone very much. I **love** eating ice-cream!

luck

Something good or bad that happens by chance.

lunch

The meal you eat in the middle of the day.

SLICED LUNCH

When the word **lunch** first appeared at the end of the 1500s, it was used to describe a thick slice of food such as bread or meat.

lungs

The two parts of your body inside your chest which fill with air when you breathe in.

Mm

machine
A tool with moving parts, which is usually powered by an engine or electricity – cars and computers are both **machines**.

magazine
A thin book with a soft cover which has pictures, photographs and short pieces of writing in it.

magician
Someone who does strange and wonderful things as if by magic.

magnet
Something that pulls objects with the metal iron in them towards it.

mail
Letters and parcels sent by post.

MAIL BAGS

The word **mail** came into English from an old German word – *malha*, meaning bag or pouch. Over time it came to mean a bag for carrying letters, and then the letters themselves.

male
A boy or a man – any animal that is not female.

mammal
An animal that feeds its young with its own milk. Humans, cats, dogs and whales are **mammals**.

mane
The long hair on the neck of a horse or a lion.

mark
1 A spot or scratch on something. There's a dirty **mark** on my shirt where I spilt soup.
2 To check how well a thing is done. Teachers **mark** homework.

marsupial
An animal whose babies are carried in a pouch in the mother's body.

Kangaroos and koalas are **marsupials**.

2 A game played between two people or teams, for example, a tennis **match**.
3 To go with something. My red hat **matches** my new red coat.

material
What things are made from. Cotton is a **material** used to make clothes. Bricks and wood are **materials** used to build houses.

maths
Short for **math**ematics. The study of numbers and shapes.

match
1 A small thin stick with a special tip which catches on fire when it is rubbed against something rough.

mean
1 Unkind, not wanting to share things.
2 To explain or show things. Dictionaries tell us what words **mean**.

measure

measure
To find out how big or heavy something is. I'm going to **measure** my little sister to find out how tall she is.

meat
The part of animals that is eaten. Beef is **meat** from a cow, for example.

medicine
Something you take when you are ill to make you feel better.

DOCTOR'S HELP

The word **medicine** came from the Latin for doctor – *medicus*.

---

meet
To come together. I say 'hello' when I **meet** a friend.

melt
When heat turns a solid into a liquid. Warm sunshine **melts** snow and it turns into water.

member
Someone who belongs to a group or a team.

memory
Remembering things. Mark has a good **memory** – he never forgets people's names.

message
Written or spoken words that are passed from one person to another. Maria sent a **message** to me saying she was ill.

metal
A hard material, such as iron, gold or silver.

method
A way of doing things. Using an index is a **method** of looking up words in a book.

microscope
A tool that makes very small things look bigger.

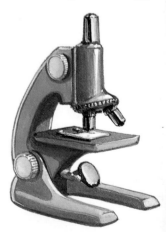

microwave
A type of short radio wave. You can cook food very quickly in a **microwave** oven.

MICRO WORDS

The first part of the words **microscope** and **microwave** came from the Greek word *mikros*, meaning small.

---

middle
The centre of something, halfway.

midnight
The middle of the night, 12 o'clock.

milk
A white liquid that mothers make in their bodies for their babies to drink. The **milk** we drink every day comes from cows.

miner
Someone who works in tunnels deep under the ground, digging out coal and metals like gold.

mineral
Any natural material found in the ground that does not come from animals or plants. All rocks are made up of **minerals**.

miniature
Very very small, tiny.

minute
A length of time. There are 60 seconds in a **minute**, and 60 **minutes** in an hour.

mirror
A special piece of glass with a shiny back to it. You can see a picture of yourself in a **mirror**.

miserable
Feeling unhappy and sad. When my cat died I was so **miserable** that I cried.

miss
1 When you do not catch or hit a thing. I **missed** the ball because I slipped and fell over.
2 To feel sad because someone is not with you.

mistake
Something that is not quite right. I went to the party on the wrong day by **mistake**.

moment
A very short period of time.

money
The special coins and pieces of paper we use to buy things.

monkey
A furry wild animal with long arms and legs, and usually a long tail.

A **miserable monkey** counting **money**.

monster
A large and frightening creature in a story book or a film.

month
A length of time. There are 12 **months** in a year and each one lasts about 4 weeks.

THE MONTHS OF THE YEAR

January	July	30 days hath September,
February	August	April, June and November.
March	September	All the rest have 31,
April	October	Excepting February clear,
May	November	Which has 28 days,
June	December	And 29 in each Leap Year.

moon
A small planet that travels around another planet. Earth's **moon** is the big bright light you see in the sky at night.

morning
The early part of the day, between night and afternoon.

mountain
A very high hill.

mouse
A very small furry animal with a long tail.

muscle
The fleshy parts under your skin are **muscles**. They are stretchy and they make you move by getting tighter or looser.

MAN OR MOUSE?

The word **muscle** came from the Latin *musculus*, meaning 'little mouse' – people thought muscles looked like little mice running about under the skin!

---

museum
A special building where interesting things from other times and places are kept for people to look at.

music
Sounds made by people singing or playing a musical instrument such as a guitar.

guitar

violin

clarinet

trumpet

recorder

53

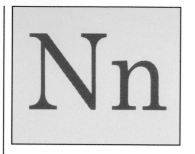

Nn

naked
Without any clothes on. When you have a bath, you are **naked**.

name
What a person, animal, place or thing is called. **Names** always begin with a capital letter. My cat's **name** is Fluffy.

narrow
Not wide. The door was so **narrow** that only one person could squeeze through at a time.

nasty
Horrid, unpleasant. This milk smells **nasty**. I think it's bad.

nation
A country and all the people who live in it. Britain is a **nation**, for example, and so is the United States of America.

nature
Everything in the world not made by people, such as plants and animals, rivers and mountains.

naughty
Behaving badly. My little sister is **naughty**. She never does what Mum tells her to.

need
When having or getting something is important. We **need** to breathe air to stay alive.

neighbour
A person who lives next door or very near to you.

nervous
Feeling worried about something. I'm a bit **nervous** about the spelling test, so I'm going to stay in to learn the words tonight.

nest
An animal's home, usually made of woven twigs and grass. Birds lay their eggs in **nests**.

newspaper
Sheets of paper printed with words and pictures, which tell you what is happening in the world. **Newspapers** come out daily or weekly.

nibble
To take very small bites when eating something.

night
The time between evening and morning, when the Sun is not in the sky and it is dark.

A mouse **nibbling nuts** at **night**.

nightmare
A frightening dream.

nocturnal
When something is only active in the night. Bats are **nocturnal** – they sleep during the day.

noise
The sound that someone or something makes. I couldn't sleep last night because of the **noise** of the traffic in the road outside our house.

FEELING SICK?
The word **noise** came to us from the French, who took it from the Latin word *nausea* – which once meant 'seasickness'!

nonsense
Silly talk or writing. It's **nonsense** to say that elephants can fly!

normal
Ordinary, how things usually are. Yesterday was a **normal** day, until a helicopter landed on the school roof!

55

nuisance

Something or someone that annoys you or gives you problems. My cat is being a real **nuisance** today – it keeps leaping up and scratching me with its claws.

number

1 A figure or word that tells you how many. For example, 1 (one) and 2 (two) are **numbers**.
2 Several. There are a **number** of books on that shelf.

nurse

Someone whose job it is to look after young babies or people who are either sick or very old.

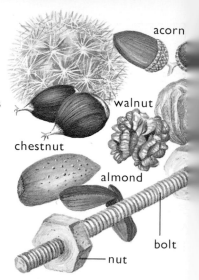

acorn
walnut
chestnut
almond
bolt
nut

nut

1 A hard fruit with a hard shell. Almonds, acorns, chest**nuts**, coco**nuts** and wal**nuts** are all **nuts**.
2 A small piece of metal with a hole in it, which screws on to a bolt to hold things together.

COUNTING WORDS		
0 zero	10 ten	20 twenty
1 one	11 eleven	30 thirty
2 two	12 twelve	40 forty
3 three	13 thirteen	50 fifty
4 four	14 fourteen	60 sixty
5 five	15 fifteen	70 seventy
6 six	16 sixteen	80 eighty
7 seven	17 seventeen	90 ninety
8 eight	18 eighteen	100 one hundred
9 nine	19 nineteen	1000 one thousand
1,000,000 one million		1,000,000,000 one billion

Oo

oasis
A place in the desert where there is water, so plants can grow.

obey
To do what you are told.

ocean
A very large sea. There are four **oceans** – the Arctic, Atlantic, Indian and Pacific **oceans**.

octopus
A sea animal with a soft body and eight arms called tentacles.

ARMS OR LEGS?

Although an **octopus** has arms, not legs, this animal's name came from the Greek words *okto* and *pous*, which mean 'eight foot'!

---

offer
1 To say you will do something for someone. 2 To invite someone to take something. My friend was thirsty, so I **offered** her a drink.

office
A room where someone works, usually with paper and books, sitting at a desk.

only
A single one, nothing or no one else. Oscar is the **only** person in our class with blonde hair – all the other children have brown or black hair.

open
Not shut. The door was **open**, so I walked straight in.

opinion
What someone thinks, their ideas or beliefs about something.

opposite
1 Not the same in any way. For example, big is the **opposite** of little.
2 On the other side. We crossed a bridge to get to the **opposite** side of the river.

orbit
To travel around something. The Moon **orbits** the Earth.

orchard
A place where fruit trees are grown.

orchestra
A large group of people playing together on lots of different musical instruments.

order
1 To tell someone that they must do something. The officer **ordered** the soldiers to stop firing.
2 To ask for something in a restaurant or a shop. I **ordered** a pizza for lunch.
3 When things are neat and tidy, and in their right place. The words in a dictionary are in alphabetical **order**.

ordinary
Normal, not special or exciting. Today is an **ordinary** day, but tomorrow we are going on a trip to the zoo.

organize
To put things in order, or to plan something so that it happens the way you want it to. Olivia is going to **organize** the disco – she'll make sure that it starts on time and that we have lots of good records to dance to.

ostrich
The largest living bird. **Ostriches** can't fly, but they can run very fast.

BIG BIRD

The ancient Greek name for the **ostrich** was *megas strouthos*, which means 'great sparrow'!

---

other
Different. Some days I drink milk for breakfast, but **other** days I have orange juice.

otter
A furry water animal which is very good at swimming and diving.

oven
The part of a cooker where food is baked or roasted.

owl
A night bird with big round eyes and a small hooked beak.

oxygen
One of the gases in the air we breathe.

SUN SHIELD

Ozone is type of **oxygen**. The ozone layer around the Earth protects us from the harmful rays given off by the Sun.

Pp

paddle
1 A pole with a flat part at one or both ends, used to move a small boat through water.
2 To walk in shallow water with bare feet.

page
One side of a piece of paper in a book, magazine or newspaper. There are 96 **pages** in this dictionary.

pain
A sore feeling in part of your body that you get when you are ill or you have hurt yourself.

paint
A coloured liquid we use to make pictures or to decorate things like walls.

pair
Two things that match or go together. You wear a **pair** of shoes.

panda
A furry animal that looks like a small black-and-white bear.

paper
Thin flat sheets of material used for writing, printing or painting on, as well as for wrapping up things like presents.

parachute
A big piece of very thin, strong material which lets people float slowly down through the air if they jump out of an aeroplane.

parcel
Something wrapped in paper and fixed with string or sticky tape, usually so it can be sent through the post.

parent
A mother or a father.

parliament
The group of people who make a country's laws.

> **LAW TALK**
>
> The word **parliament** came from *parlement*, a French word which means a 'talk' or a 'discussion'.

parrot
A brightly coloured bird with a strong hooked beak. Some **parrots** can learn to copy sounds and words.

passenger
Someone who takes a ride in a car, bus, train, boat or aeroplane – not the driver.

passport
A special book with your photograph in it, as well as your name and other information about you. You usually need to show your **passport** when you travel abroad to other countries.

pasta
An Italian food made from flour which comes in lots of different shapes, from little shells to long thin sticks called spaghetti.

patient
1 Someone who is being looked after by a doctor or a nurse.
2 Being able to wait without getting cross. I have to be **patient** with my little sister – she can't do everything as quickly as I can.

pavement
A hard raised path along the edge of a road.

peace
1 Calm and quiet.
2 A time when there is no war or fighting between countries.

penguin

A large black-and-white seabird. **Penguins** cannot fly, but they can swim very well.

people

Human beings – girls and boys, women and men. There are billions of **people** in the world, but each one is different and special.

person

A woman, man or child – a human being.

petrol

A liquid made from oil. When **petrol** is burnt in a car engine, it gives the car the power to move.

photocopier

A machine that copies words or pictures on to paper.

photograph

A picture taken with a camera.

LIGHT WRITING

There was no such word as **photograph** until 1839, the year in which the first photographs were made. It comes from two Greek words – *photo* meaning 'light', and *graphos* meaning 'written'.

photosynthesis

The way in which the energy in sunlight is used by plants to make food in their leaves.

picnic

A meal that you take with you and eat out of doors, often in the country or at the beach.

piece

1 A bit or part of something. I can't finish this jigsaw because some of the **pieces** are missing.
2 To mend or put something together.

pilot
Someone who flies an aeroplane or guides a ship safely into harbour.

OARSMAN
Ships were invented thousands of years before aeroplanes, and the word **pilot** came from the Greek word *pedon*, meaning 'oar'. The term aircraft **pilot** was first used in 1907.

pirate
A sailor who robs ships at sea.

A **pirate** with a **parrot** on his shoulder.

pity
A feeling of sadness for someone or something.

planet
A huge round object in Space that goes around a star. Earth is a **planet** – it goes around the star we call the Sun.

plant
1 A living thing that is not an animal. Unlike animals, **plants** make their own food using the energy in sunlight.
2 To put seeds or plants in the earth so that they grow.

plastic
A light material which is not easily broken. **Plastic** is used to make all sorts of things, from toys to raincoats.

please
1 To make someone happy.
2 We also say '**please**' when we ask for something politely.

63

poem

poem
A special piece of writing in which the words are chosen for their sound as well as their meaning. **Poems** often have short lines, and the last words of the lines sometimes rhyme.

poison
Something that makes people very sick or even kills them.

police
Men and women whose job is making sure that people obey the law.

polite
Well-behaved, not rude. It is **polite** to say 'thank you' when someone gives you something.

pollute
To spoil the air, the land or the water by making it dirty. Some factory wastes **pollute** the air and the water.

popular
Liked by a lot of people. Pete is very **popular** – everyone in our class likes him a lot.

POPULAR WORD

The words **people**, **population** and **popular** all came from the Latin word for people – *populus*.

population
All the people living in a place – a town, a city, a country or the world.

power
1 The strength or energy to make a thing happen. Cars get the **power** to move from petrol.
2 Control over other people. The queen had more **power** than anyone else in her country.

practise
To do something lots of times so that you get better at it.

precious
To be worth a lot. The baby was very **precious** to her mum and dad.

prehistoric
Things that happened long ago, before writing was invented and people started recording things by writing them down.

present
1 Something you give to someone. People give **presents** at Christmas.
2 Now, at this time. There are two boys called Paul in my class at **present** – there was only one last year.

president
The head of a country or an organization.

pretend
To act as though you are someone or something you are not.

I'm going to **pretend** to be a lion in the play.

pretty
Nice-looking, attractive.

PRETTY CLEVER

The word **pretty** once meant 'crafty' or 'clever'. People began using it to mean 'nice-looking' in the 1400s.

prey
An animal that is hunted and killed by other animals. Mice are cats' **prey**, for example.

65

print
1 Letters that are not joined together.
2 To use a machine to put words or pictures on paper. This book was **printed** on a machine.

prison
A building where people are locked up when they break the law by doing something bad.

private
Something that is only for one person or for one group of people.

prize
A reward for doing something well.

promise
To say that you will do something. My friend says she'll tell me a secret if I **promise** not to tell it to anyone.

puppet
A kind of doll that can be made to move. You put your hand inside some **puppets**. Others have strings to pull.

DOLL AND DOG

The word **puppet** came from *pupa*, which is Latin for a 'girl' or a 'doll'. Our word for a young dog, puppy, also came from *pupa*.

puzzle
Something hard to understand or sort out, like a jigsaw **puzzle**.

python
A large snake with a very powerful body.

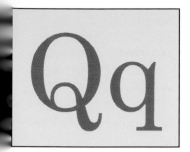

Qq

quarrel
To argue with a person in an angry way. If my brother and I **quarrel**, we always make friends again afterwards.

quarry
A place where stone is cut or blasted out of the ground.

queen
1 A woman who is the head of a country, or the wife of a king.
2 A large female ant, bee or wasp that can lay eggs. There is often only one **queen** in each group of insects.

question
What you ask when you want to find out about something. 'Which animal has a long trunk and big tusks?' is a **question**. 'An elephant' is the answer.

queue
A line of people or traffic waiting for something.

QUICK OR DEAD
The word **quick** once meant 'alive'. People began using it to mean 'fast' in the 1200s.

quick
Fast or speedy, not slow. Calculators are very **quick** at adding up sums – it takes me much longer if I work sums out in my head.

quiet
Not noisy, peaceful. Please turn up the radio – the music is so **quiet** that I can't hear it.

quiz
A game with lots of questions.

Rr

rabbit
A small furry wild animal which has long ears and a very short fluffy tail.

radio
A machine that receives messages sent through the air in the form of a special type of energy called **radio** waves. The **radio** changes the messages into words and music so that we can listen to them.

rail
1 A bar or pole used to support something, or which is part of a fence. **2** One of the metal bars that trains run on.

railway
A way of carrying passengers and goods in trains that run on rails.

raise
To lift something up or make it higher. You **raise** one foot after the other when you climb the stairs.

reach
1 To arrive somewhere. We'll have a rest when we **reach** the top of the mountain. **2** To stretch out towards something. Please pass me that book – I can't **reach** it from here.

MAKING WAVES

The first **radio** message was sent by Guglielmo Marconi in 1887. At first the new machine was known as a wireless, because it sent messages through the air instead of along a wire. The word **radio** was first used in the 1900s.

read
To look at words and know what they mean.

I'm **reading** a letter I **received** from a friend.

reason
Why or how something happens. The **reason** I'm late today is that I missed the bus.

receive
To get something that has been given or sent.

record
1 A round flat piece of plastic that makes music when you play it on a machine called a **record** player.
2 To set something down so that it will be remembered.

EARLY RECORDS

One of the first tunes to be put on a **record** was *Twinkle, Twinkle, Little Star*.

---

relative
Someone who belongs to your family, like your mother or your uncle.

remember
Not to forget, to hold things in your mind. I must **remember** to take my sports things to school today, because we're playing baseball this afternoon.

reptile
A land animal with a dry scaly skin. **Reptiles** lay large eggs with leathery shells. Snakes and crocodiles are **reptiles**.

rescue
To save someone or something from danger.

responsible
In charge of something. Rob is **responsible** for the puppy – he has to look after it and teach it not to be naughty.

restaurant
A place where you can buy and eat meals.

return
1 To come back.
2 To give something back. Please **return** my book when you've finished reading it.

reward
A present for doing something good.

Mum gave me a **reward** for **rescuing** our cat.

rhinoceros
A large wild animal with a thick skin. Some **rhinoceroses** have two horns on their nose, others only have one.

rhyme
When words sound similar. Egg and leg **rhyme**, for example.

rhythm
The pattern of beats in music or a poem.

right
1 Good, true, correct. When I am not sure about the **right** way to spell a word, I look it up in a dictionary.
2 The opposite of left. You have a **right** hand and a left hand.

river
A large amount of moving fresh water which flows into a lake or the sea.

road

A type of long hard path, wide enough for cars and other vehicles to drive along it.

robot

A machine built to do some of the jobs that people usually do.

SLAVE LABOUR

The word **robot** came into the English language in the 1920s, after it was used in a play by the Czech writer Karel Ĉapek. In Czech, *robota* means 'work done by slaves'.

rocket

1 A firework on the end of a stick, which shoots into the air when lit.
2 Something used to launch spacecraft and special types of weapon.

rough

1 Not smooth or flat. Because the road was very **rough**, our car ride was very bumpy.
2 Not gentle.

rubber

1 A strong stretchy material. Car tyres are made of **rubber**, and so are **rubber** bands.
2 A small piece of **rubber** or plastic used to rub out pencil marks.

rubbish

Unwanted or leftover things that are thrown away, such as waste food or empty tins.

runway

A type of long hard path that aeroplanes land on and take off from.

Ss

safe

1 Not in any danger. The mouse is **safe** inside its hole because the cat can't reach it there.

2 A strong metal cupboard with special locks, which is used to store money and valuable things.

sailor

Someone who works on a ship or a boat.

sandwich

1 Two slices of bread with food such as jam or cheese in between them.

2 To squash things together.

A LORD'S LUNCH

Sandwiches were invented in the 1700s, by the English Earl of Sandwich.

satellite

Anything that orbits a planet. The Earth's **satellites** are the Moon and many different Space machines.

scare

To frighten someone. Big dogs **scare** me – I'm worried they'll bite me.

school

1 A place where children learn about themselves and the world around them.

2 A large group of fish.

science

The study of things in nature, from ourselves to the stars and the planets.

scissors

A tool with two blades that cut when they close together. Each blade has a handle with a hole for a finger or thumb.

scream
To make a loud high cry because of fear or pain. I **screamed** when I thought I saw a ghost!

seal
1 A sea animal with smooth furry skin.
2 To close something by sticking it together. You **seal** envelopes before you post them.

search
To look carefully for something.

season
One of the four parts of each year. Most areas of the world have four **seasons** – spring, summer, autumn and winter.

secret
Something that very few people know about. I won't tell anyone where Sam is hiding because it's our **secret**.

selfish
Thinking only about yourself, not caring about other people. Mum says I'm **selfish** because I ate all the biscuits and I didn't offer them to anyone.

sense
1 One of the ways our bodies find out what is happening around us.
2 The meaning of something. I can't make **sense** of this book because it's written in Russian.

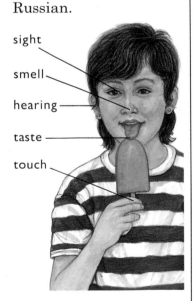

sight
smell
hearing
taste
touch

Most people have five **senses** – hearing, sight, smell, taste and touch.

sentence
A group of words that mean something. When a **sentence** is written down, it begins with a capital letter and ends with a full stop (.), a question mark (?), or an exclamation mark (!).

shake
To move quickly up and down or from side to side. You **shake** your head from side to side to show you mean 'no', and up and down to show you mean 'yes'.

sheep
A farm animal with a thick woolly coat.

AS SHY AS SHEEP
The word **sheep**ish can be used to describe a shy person – someone who behaves rather like a **sheep**!

shell
The hard outside covering of an egg or a nut, or of an animal such as a snail or a tortoise.

shark
A type of large fish that lives in the sea and has very sharp teeth. Some **sharks** attack people.

sharp
When something has a finely pointed edge or end which is good for cutting things. Scissors are **sharp**, for example.

silent
Making no noise. When our teacher asks us to be **silent**, she wants us stop talking and be quiet.

similar
Like, but not exactly the same. Out shirts are **similar**, but mine is red and yours is blue.

sing
To make music with your voice.

skateboard
A small board with wheels, on which you can ride or do tricks.

skeleton
All the bones inside the bodies of people and other animals.

skid
To slip by mistake. Cars may **skid** on icy roads.

skin
1 The outer covering of our bodies.
2 The outer covering of a fruit or a vegetable.

skip
1 To bounce along making little hops and jumps.
2 A large metal container for rubbish.

sky
The space around the Earth. You can usually see the Moon and stars in the **sky** at night.

BAG OF BONES

The word **skeleton** came from the Greek word *skeletos*, which means 'dried up' – a **skeleton** is what is left after an animal dies and the rest of its body dries up and rots away.

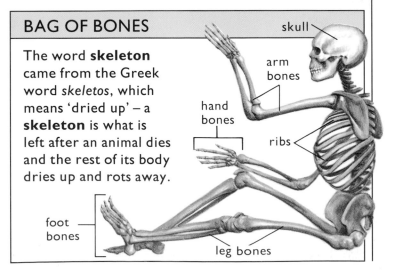

skull
arm bones
hand bones
ribs
foot bones
leg bones

skyscraper

skyscraper
A very tall building.

sleep
When you shut your eyes and go into such a deep rest that you do not know what is going on around you.

slide
1 To move smoothly over something. You can **slide** on ice.
2 A big toy that you **slide** down.

slow
Not fast or quick.

small
Not big, little.

smooth
Flat and even, without any lumps, holes or rough bits.

snail
A small animal with a soft body and a hard shell on its back.

CRAWLERS
The words **snail** and **snake** came from an ancient German word which meant 'to crawl'.

snake
A long thin animal without any legs.

sneeze
To blow air out of your nose very quickly. You usually **sneeze** a lot when you have a cold.

sniff
To take air in through your nose very quickly.

snore
To breathe very noisily when you are sleeping.

snow
Soft white bits of frozen water which fall from the sky in very cold weather.

soil
The earth in which plants live and grow.

solar
To do with the Sun. **Solar** energy can be used to make electricity to heat water.

somersault
A movement you do by turning head over heels.

sorry
Feeling sad or unhappy about something. Steve said he was **sorry** that he broke the window.

sound
Anything you hear.

space
1 Empty, where there is nothing. I can't find a **space** on the shelf to put this book.
2 Above the Earth, where there is no air. The Sun, Moon, planets and stars are in **Space**.

spaceship
A special vehicle for travelling in Space.

speak
To talk, to say things.

special
1 Something that is different, better, or more important than other things of its kind. Most mice are brown, so white mice are **special**.
2 Something that has just one use. A hammer is a **special** tool for banging in nails.

species
A group of animals or plants that are alike in some way. For example, panthers, tigers, leopards and lions are all **species** of cat.

speed
How fast or slow a thing travels. Spaceships travel at great **speed**.

spell

spell
1 To put the letters of a word in the correct order. You can use a dictionary to check how to **spell** words.
2 Magic words. In the story, the wicked witch said a **spell** that turned the prince into a frog.

spider
A little animal with eight legs. Most **spiders** spin sticky webs which they use to trap insects to eat.

sport
A game such as tennis in which you move about a lot. In many **sports**, two teams play against each other.

swimming

basketball

tennis

baseball

football

78

squeeze
To press something very tightly.

squirrel
A small furry animal with a long bushy tail.

star
1 A ball of burning gas in Space. Our Sun is a **star**, and so are the thousands of bright shining lights you see in the sky at night.
2 A famous singer, actor or sportsperson.

STAR SIGNS

The Greek word for **star** is *aster*. The English words asterisk, a star shape (*), and astronomy, the study of stars, both came from *aster*.

stare
To look hard and for a long time at something.

start
To begin. I can't speak French at present, but I'm going to **start** learning it next term.

station
1 A building where trains or buses stop for passengers.
2 A building used by people such as the police or firefighters.
3 In Australia, a large sheep or cattle farm.

steal
To take something that belongs to someone else without asking them.

still
Very quiet, not moving. The air was so **still** I couldn't fly my kite.

stink
To smell bad.

storm
Very bad weather, with strong winds and heavy rain, and sometimes thunder and lightning.

story
Something written or spoken that tells you about things that have happened. A **story** can be real or made up.

straight
Not bent or crooked. You can use a ruler to draw a **straight** line.

stream
A small river.

street
A road with buildings on both sides.

string
The thin cord that we use to tie things together.

strong
Not weak, someone or something with great power. The wind was so **strong** that it blew all the trees down.

study
1 To spend time reading and learning about something.
2 A room used for reading, writing and thinking.

submarine
A ship that can travel under water.

Sun
The big bright star in the sky that gives us heat and light.

SUN WORDS

The word **Sun** is used to make many other words in English. **Sun**rise is the time when the Sun rises, for example, and **sun**set is when the Sun goes down. A **sun**flower is orange and looks a little bit like the Sun.

supermarket
A very large shop where all sorts of different things are sold.

supersonic
Faster than the speed of sound. Concorde is a **supersonic** aeroplane.

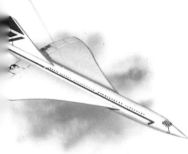

supper
The last meal of the day, which is eaten in the evening.

surface
The outside or top part of something. The spaceship landed on the **surface** of the Moon.

surprise
Something you do not expect to happen.

swallow
1 A small bird with a forked tail.
2 To make food or drink go down your throat.

swap
To change one thing for another. I don't like this blue t-shirt, so I'm going to take it back and **swap** it for a yellow one.

sweet
Something that tastes as if it has honey or sugar in it.

swing
1 To move backwards and forwards.
2 A hanging seat that you sit on and move back and forth.

synthesiser
A type of computer that can make all sorts of different sounds, from words to music.

Tt

tadpole
A very young frog or toad. **Tadpoles** live in water. They do not have any legs and they swim about like fish.

tail
1 The part that grows out of the back end of some animals' bodies.
2 To follow close behind. The police **tailed** the thieves' getaway car.

take
To pick something up and hold it or carry it somewhere. I'm going to **take** my swimsuit with me to the seaside.

tale
A **tale** is a story.

talk
To say something. I like **talking** to my friend on the telephone.

tall
Not short, high. Giraffes are so **tall** that they can eat the tops of trees.

tame
Not wild. **Tame** animals are not afraid of people and will not hurt them.

tanker
A ship or lorry used to carry gas or liquids.

taxi
A car with a driver that you pay to drive you somewhere.

teach
To show or tell a person how to do something. My dad is going to **teach** me to swim.

team
A group of people who work or play together.

tease
To make fun of someone, often in an unkind way.

teenager
Someone between the ages of thir**teen** and nine**teen**.

telephone
A machine that allows people to talk to each other across long distances. A **telephone** turns speech into electrical signals which travel along wires.

telescope
A tube-like tool with special glass and mirrors inside it that make faraway things look nearer and larger.

television
A machine that can receive and show pictures and sounds sent through the air as radio waves.

TELE WORDS

The first part of the words **telephone**, **telescope** and **television** came from the Greek word *tele*, which means 'far off'. TV is short for the word **television**, which was first used in 1909.

television

telephone

telescope

temperature

temperature
How hot or cold a thing is. The **temperature** of your body is usually about 37°C.

tent
A type of little house made of material, which people sleep in when camping. **Tents** are held up by poles and ropes.

STRETCHERS

The word **tent** came from the Latin *tentum*, which itself came from *pelles tendere*, meaning 'to stretch out skins'. The earliest **tents** were animal skins stretched out over wooden poles.

tentacle
One of the long snake-like arms of an animal such as an octopus.

terrible
Very bad, awful. The film was **terrible**. I was so bored that I fell asleep in the cinema!

texture
The way something feels. The **texture** of your skin is soft and smooth.

thank
You **thank** people when you are pleased or grateful for something they have said or they have done for you.

theatre
A special building where people go to see shows and plays.

thief
Someone who steals things that belong to other people.

think
1 To work out things in your mind. You have to **think** very hard to do a crossword.
2 To believe something is true. I **think** that's the right answer, but I'm not sure.

thirsty
You are **thirsty** when you want a drink.

thunder
The loud crashing noise you sometimes hear during a storm.

tiger
A type of large wild cat with an orangy brown and black striped coat.

time
What we measure in seconds, minutes, hours, days, months and years.

toad
A frog-like animal. Most **toads** have shorter back legs than frogs do and their skins are rougher. **Toads** usually crawl on land. Frogs leap about.

today
This day, the one you are living in.

tomorrow
The next day, the day after today.

tonight
The night of this day.

tool
Something that helps you to do a job.

MEASURING TIME
There are: 60 seconds in a minute 60 minutes in an hour 24 hours in a day 28–31 days in a month 12 months in a year

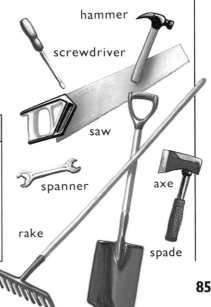

hammer

screwdriver

saw

spanner

axe

rake

spade

tooth

tooth
One of the hard white things in your mouth that you use for chewing.

tortoise
A slow-moving land animal with a thick shell on its body.

tough
1 Very strong, very hard to cut or break. The meat was so **tough** that I couldn't chew it.
2 Very difficult. It was a **tough** race, and our team nearly lost.

town
A large group of houses and other buildings. A **town** is larger than a village and smaller than a city.

tractor
A farm vehicle used for pulling things.

traffic
The cars and other vehicles that travel on roads, in the air or on water.

train
1 An engine that pulls railway coaches with people in them, or goods wagons.
2 To teach an animal or a person how to do something. I am **training** my dog to come when I call it.

transparent
Seethrough, like glass.

travel
To go from one place to another. I **travel** to school on the bus.

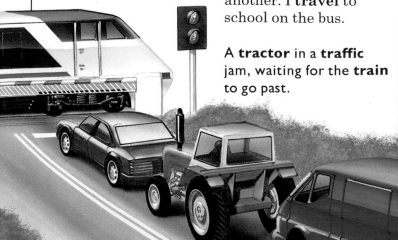

A **tractor** in a **traffic** jam, waiting for the **train** to go past.

treasure
A store of things worth a lot of money, such as gold or jewels. The pirates buried their **treasure** on the island.

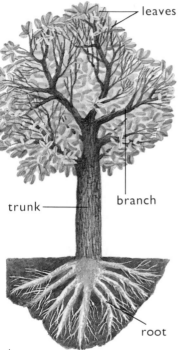

leaves
branch
trunk
root

tree
The largest of all plants. **Trees** have a woody stem called a trunk.

triangle
1 A flat shape with three straight sides.
2 A musical instrument made of metal bent into the shape of a **triangle**.

trouble
When something makes you worry and feel unhappy. I'm having **trouble** with my homework tonight – it's really difficult.

truck
A lorry or railway wagon with an open top.

true
Correct, real. It's a **true** story – I'm not making it up or telling lies.

tunnel
A long hole that has been dug underground or through a hill.

turtle
A water animal whose body is protected by a hard shell.

twins
Two children born to the same mother at the same time.

Uu

ugly
Not pretty or beautiful.

umbrella
Something you hold over your head to keep the rain off. An **umbrella** is made of cloth or plastic stretched over a frame you can open or close.

SUNSHADE

Umbrellas were invented to shade people from the Sun, but later came to be used as protection from rain. The word **umbrella** came from *ombrella* – Italian for 'little shadow'.

umpire
The person who makes sure that players obey the rules of games such as tennis and football.

understand
To know what things mean or how things work. I **understand** maps. I can use them to find my way about.

unicorn
An imaginary animal with a long horn in the middle of its forehead, and a white horse's body, a deer's hooves and a lion's tail.

uniform
Special clothes worn by people to show they belong to the same group.

A nurse in **uniform** carrying an **umbrella**.

UN-WORDS

When words have **un** in front of them, they often mean the opposite. To **un**dress means 'to take clothes off', for example. **Un**tidy means 'not tidy', and **un**happy means 'not happy'.

universe
The whole of Space and everything in it – the planets, the stars, everything.

university
A place where people can carry on studying after they leave school.

upset
1 Not very happy. I was **upset** by the bad news.
2 To knock something over. When I **upset** my drink, it spilt all over the table.

urgent
When something is so important that it needs to be done at once. The job was **urgent**, so I had to drop everything and do it straightaway.

useful
If a thing is **useful**, it helps you in some way. I found that book really **useful** when I was doing my homework.

useless
Not useful, no good to anyone. A broken watch is **useless**.

89

Vv

valley
The low land between hills or mountains. Rivers often flow through **valleys**.

valuable
1 Worth a lot of money.
2 Useful or important. Your help in getting to the hospital was most **valuable** to me.

vanish
To go suddenly out of sight or view. My friend **vanished** into the mist – one minute I could see her walking in front of me, the next I couldn't.

vegetable
A plant that is grown for food, such as carrots or peas. **Vegetables** taste less sweet than the plants we call fruit.

beans

peas

green pepper

mushroom

onion

carrot

potato

courgette

cucumber

cabbage

cauliflower

PLANT EATER

Someone who eats **vegetables**, but not meat or fish, is called a vegetarian.

vehicle
Any machine used to carry people or goods from once place to another. Cars and buses are **vehicles**.

vibrate
To move very quickly backwards and forwards. Hitting the skin of a drum with a stick makes it **vibrate**.

video
A machine that records pictures and sounds from a television set or through a special camera on to **video**tape.

village
A small town.

violent
Very strong and rough. A **violent** storm blew the roof right off the house.

visit
To go and see someone. I went to **visit** my uncle when he was in hospital.

voice
The sound you make when you speak or sing.

volcano
An opening in the Earth's surface through which hot melted rock and gases sometimes shoot out.

FIRE MOUNTAIN

Volcanoes get their name from the Roman god of fire, Volcanus or Vulcan.

vote
To show that you have chosen someone or something. I'm going to **vote** for Veronica to be team captain.

voyage
A long journey by sea or through Space.

vulture
A large bird that feeds on dead animals. **Vultures** don't have feathers on their heads.

Ww

wait
To stay in one place until something happens. I **waited** outside the station until Dad came to collect me.

walk
To move along, putting one foot in front of the other.

wash
To clean something – either with water, or with soap and water.

weather
Sunshine, rain, wind or clouds, hot or cold – what things are like outside.

week
A length of time. There are seven days in a **week**, and 52 **weeks** in a year.

weigh
To find out how heavy something is.

whale
A large sea animal. The blue **whale** is the largest animal that has ever lived – it is even larger than the biggest dinosaurs were!

watch
1 To look at. We **watch** films at the cinema or on television.
2 A little clock you wear on your wrist to tell you the time.

HUGE FUN

If you are really enjoying yourself, you can say you are having 'a **whale** of a time'.

whisper
To speak very quietly.
I am **whispering**
because I don't want
anyone else to hear.

whole
All of something. I read
the **whole** book, from
beginning to end.

wicked
Very bad or naughty.

witch
A woman in stories who
uses magic to make
things happen.

wobble
To move from side to
side like a jelly.

woman
A grown-up female
human.

work
To do a job. Farmers
work on the land,
growing plants and
looking after animals.

world
The Earth and all the
things on and in it.

worry
To be upset or troubled.
I don't want to **worry**
you, but I think I've
broken your watch.

write
To put numbers, letters
or words on paper.

wrong
Not correct. I got lost on
the way home because I
took the **wrong** turning.

WICKED WITCH

In Old English the
word for **witch** was
wicce, while the word
for a wizard, or male
witch, was *wicca*.
Wicked came from
wicca, and it meant
'wizard-like' at first.

Xx Yy Zz

x-ray
A type of energy that can't be seen, which allows doctors to take special photographs of people's insides.

yacht
A boat used for sailing or racing.

yawn
You **yawn** when you are tired or bored. You open your mouth very wide and take in a deep breath of air.

year
The time it takes for the Earth to travel around the Sun. There are 365 days, 52 weeks, and 12 months in a **year**.

yesterday
The day before today.

yoghurt
A creamy food made from milk.

young
1 Not old.
2 Baby animals.

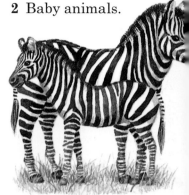

A **zebra** with its **young**.

zebra
A wild African animal that looks like a horse with a stripey coat.

zip
A **zip** has two sets of teeth that lock together to fasten clothes or bags.

zoo
A place where wild animals are kept so that people can look at them.

ANIMAL HOME

Zoo is a short form of **zoo**logical. This came from the Greek word for 'animal' – *zoion*.

94

INDEX

This index gives page numbers for words that are either illustrated or in boxes, but which are not included as main entries in the dictionary.

A
acorn 56
almond 56
ankle 12
apple 29
April 52
arm 12, 73
August 52
axe 85

B
banana 29
baseball 78
basketball 78
beans 90
belt 18
billion 56
blue 19
bolt 56
boot 18
bracelet 38
branch 87
brooch 38

C
cabbage 90
calf 12
cap 18
carnation 28
carrot 90

cauliflower 90
cherry 29
chestnut 56
chest 12
chin 12
clarinet 53
courgette 90
cucumber 90

D
daffodil 28
December 52

E
earrings 38
ears 12
eight 56
eighteen 56
eighty 56
elbow 12
eleven 56
eyes 12

F
February 52
fifteen 56
fifty 56
fingers 12
five 56
foot 12, 73

football 78
forty 56
four 56
fourteen 56
Friday 21

G
grapes 29
green 19
  pepper 90
guitar 53

H
hair 12
hammer 85
hand 12, 73
head 12
hearing 73
hundred 56

I
indigo 19

J
jacket 18
January 52
jeans 18
jumper 18
July 52
June 52

K
knee 12

L
leaves 87
leg 12, 73
lemon 29
lily 28

M
March 52
May 52
million 56
Monday 21
mouth 12
mushroom 90

N
neck 12
necklace 38
nine 56
nineteen 56
ninety 56
nose 12
November 52
nut 56

O
October 52
one 56
onion 90
orange 19, 29

P
pansy 28
pear 29
peas 90
poppy 28

potato 90
pupa 16

R
rake 85
recorder 53
red 19
ribs 73
ring 38
root 87
rose 28

S
Saturday 21
saw 85
scarf 18
screwdriver 85
September 52
seven 56
seventeen 56
seventy 56
shirt 18
shoe 18
shoulders 12
sight 73
six 56
sixteen 56
sixty 56
skirt 18
skull 73
smell 73
socks 18
spade 85
spanner 85
stomach 12
Sunday 21
swimming 78

T
taste 73
ten 56
tennis 78
thigh 12
thirteen 56
thirty 56
thousand 56
three 56
Thursday
tights 18
toes 12
tomato 29
touch 73
trumpet 53
trunk 87
Tuesday 21
tulip 28
twelve 56
twenty 56
two 56

V
violet 19
violin 53

W
waist 12
walnut 56
Wednesday
wrist 12

Y
yellow 19

Z
zero 56